DC COMICS™
SUPER HEROES

THE SCIENCE BEHIND

BATMAN'S

UNIFORM

by
Agnieszka Biskup

BATMAN created by
Bob Kane with Bill Finger

SCIENCE BEHIND
BATMAN

CAPSTONE PRESS
a capstone imprint

Published by Capstone Press in 2016
A Capstone Imprint
1710 Roe Crest Drive
North Mankato, Minnesota 56003
www.mycapstone.com

STAR36691

Library of Congress Cataloging-in-Publication Data
Names: Biskup, Agnieszka, author.
Title: Science behind Batman's uniform / by Agnieszka Biskup.
Description: North Mankato, Minnesota : Capstone Press, 2016. | 2016 | Series: DC super heroes.
   Science behind Batman | Audience: Ages 7-9. | Audience: K to grade 3. | Includes
   bibliographical references and index.
Identifiers: LCCN 2016002662| ISBN 9781515720317 (library binding) | ISBN 9781515720393 (paperback)
   | ISBN 9781515720430 (ebook (pdf))
Subjects: LCSH: Batman (Fictitious character)—Juvenile literature. | Body armor—Juvenile
   literature. | Crime prevention—Technological innovations—Juvenile literature.
Classification: LCC HV8073 .B5545 2017 | DDC 600—dc23
LC record available at http://lccn.loc.gov/2016002662

Summary: Explores the real-world science and engineering connections to the features of Batman's Batsuit.

Editorial Credits
Christopher Harbo, editor; Hilary Wacholz, designer; Wanda Winch, media researcher;
Tori Abraham, production specialist

Artwork by Luciano Vecchio and Ethen Beavers

Photo Credits
Alamy: Jeff Mood, 9 (right); Dreamstime: Lawrence Weslowski Jr., 13 (left); Getty Images: Denver Post/Ernie
Leyba, 15 (l); Glow Images: Science Faction/SuperStock, 13 (r); NASA, 7 (bottom left); Newscom: ZUMA Press/
ChinaFotoPress, 20; Shutterstock: TFoxFoto, 9 (l), Fotokostic, 10, 501room, 10 (inset), Alexandra Lande, 19; U.S.
Navy: PH2 John L. Beeman, 7 (top right), MC3 Billy Ho, 16, Lt. Troy Wilcox, 17; Wikimedia: J. Glover, Atlanta,
Georgia, 15 (r)

Printed in China.
007727

TABLE OF CONTENTS

INTRODUCTION
BEHIND THE BATSUIT

Most super heroes have incredible powers. But not Batman. He fights crime with science and engineering. His Batsuit is loaded with amazing **technology**. Best of all, the science behind his suit is found in our world too.

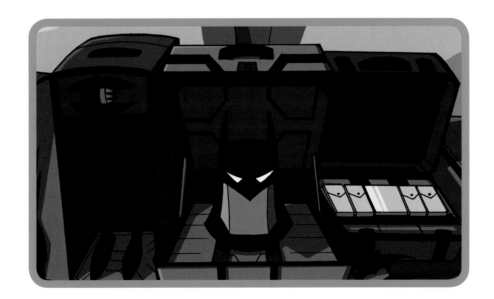

technology—the use of science to do practical things, such as designing complex machines

Batman's suit protects him from deadly impacts.

Batman's mask protects his head and hides his identity.

Batman's Utility Belt contains many gadgets and weapons.

Batman's cape allows him to glide through the air.

Batman's suit keeps him warm and protects against fiery explosions.

5

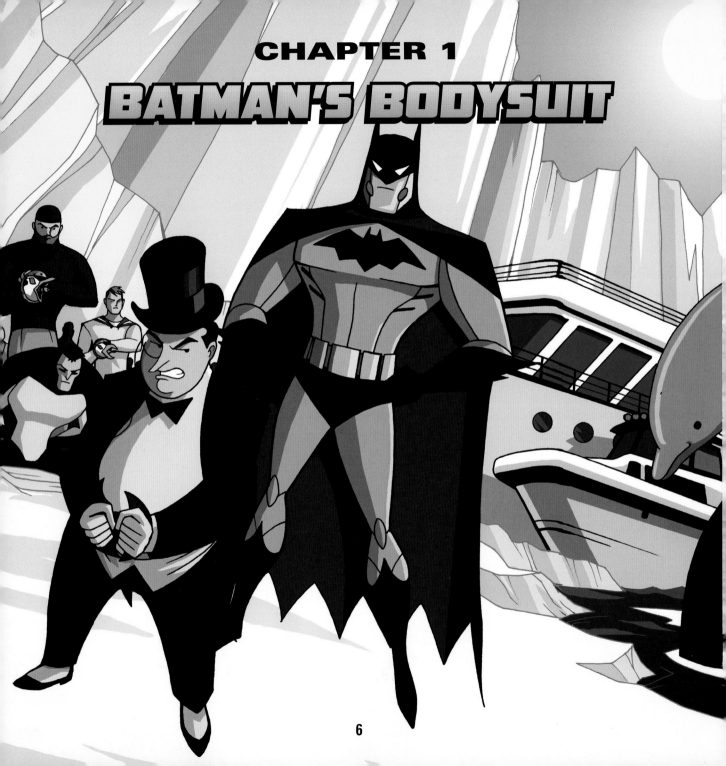

Batman's **bodysuit** keeps him warm during cold nights. In our world, **neoprene** bodysuits help divers stay warm. The rubber-like material contains tiny gas bubbles. These bubbles help stop heat from leaving a diver's body.

A Navy diver wears a neoprene wetsuit to stay warm in the water.

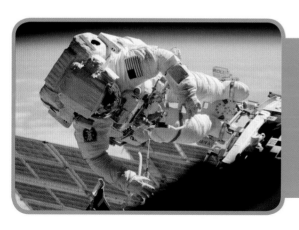

FACT

Spacesuits have layers that protect astronauts from heat, cold, and flying objects.

bodysuit—a close-fitting one-piece article of clothing, typically worn for sports

neoprene—a strong, waterproof material sometimes used to make wetsuits

Batman's suit protects him from fiery explosions.

Nomex in a firefighter's gear protects against the heat of a fire.

In the real world, Nomex gear protects race car drivers and firefighters against burns. This material has special **fibers** that thicken when fire touches them. The swelling fibers protect the skin from heat.

FACT

Stunt people wear Nomex suits to film fiery scenes in movies.

fiber—a long, thin thread of material, such as cotton, wool, or silk

The Batsuit helps shield the Caped Crusader from deadly **impacts**. In our world, police officers wear bulletproof vests made from Kevlar. This fabric gets its strength from tightly woven fibers.

Inside police vests are many layers of tightly woven Kevlar.

impact—the striking of one thing against another
ceramic—made of materials that are hardened by heat

FACT

Some body armor
has **ceramic** plates.
These plates are as
strong as steel, but
are much lighter.

CHAPTER 2

THE CAPED CRUSADER'S COWL

Batman's **cowl** hides his face and protects his head. In real life, soldiers and athletes protect their heads with helmets. Their helmets have hard shells and soft foam liners. A hard shell spreads the force of an impact over a large area. A foam liner **absorbs** the impact's energy.

Military helmets often include Kevlar to protect against bullets.

A NASCAR pit crew member wears a helmet to protect against accidents during a race.

cowl—a hood or long hooded cloak

absorb—to soak up

The ears of Batman's cowl carry microphones for spying on villains. In our world, **parabolic** microphones help with long-distance listening. These bowl-shaped devices can record sounds up to 300 yards (274 meters) away.

A parabolic microphone picks up the sounds of a game.

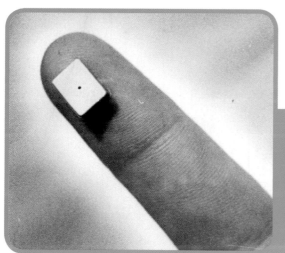

FACT

Bugs are hidden microphones that secretly pick up sounds. They can be as small as pencil erasers.

parabolic—shaped like a bowl

Night-vision lenses help Batman see in the dark. Real night-vision gear uses either **thermal** imaging or image **enhancement**. Thermal imaging lets you see heat given off by objects. Image enhancement boosts available light to make objects look brighter.

A soldier tests the settings on night-vision goggles.

Night-vision goggles with image enhancement show objects in green. Why? Because our eyes can see more shades of green than any other color.

thermal—having to do with heat

enhancement—making something better or greater

CHAPTER 3
THE DARK KNIGHT'S CAPE

Similar to a hang glider, Batman's cape helps him glide through the air. A hang glider is a curved, triangle-shaped wing. It rises when air flows over its surface to create **lift**. Hang glider pilots can easily soar 100 miles (161 kilometers) in a single flight.

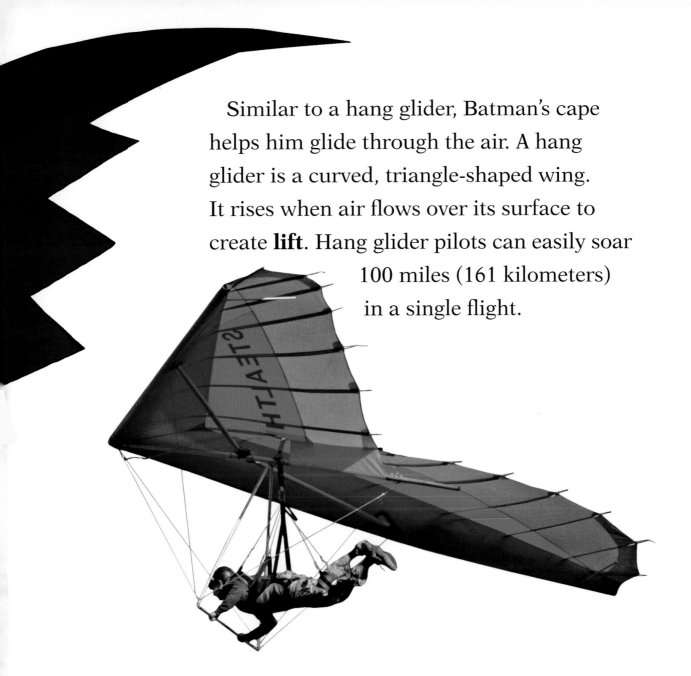

lift—the upward force of air that causes an object to fly

Some people use wingsuits to glide like Batman. These suits have webbing between the legs and under the arms. During a jump, air fills the webbing to help wingsuiters glide like flying squirrels. Wingsuiters then use parachutes to land safely.

A wingsuiter glides through the air above Tianmen Mountain in China.

The Batsuit seems like a simple
disguise, but it's really the ultimate
super hero body armor. The real
science behind it is as amazing as
the Caped Crusader it protects.

GLOSSARY

absorb (ab-ZORB)—to soak up

bodysuit (BOD-ee-soot)—a close-fitting one-piece article of clothing, typically worn for sports

ceramic (suh-RA-mik)—made of materials that are hardened by heat

cowl (KOUL)—a hood or long hooded cloak

enhancement (en-HANSS-muhnt)—making something better or greater

fiber (FY-buhr)—a long, thin thread of material, such as cotton, wool, or silk

impact (IM-pakt)—the striking of one thing against another

lift (LIFT)—the upward force of air that causes an object to fly

neoprene (NEE-uh-preen)—a strong, waterproof material sometimes used to make wetsuits

parabolic (pa-ruh-BAH-lik)—shaped like a bowl

technology (tek-NOL-uh-jee)—the use of science to do practical things, such as designing complex machines

thermal (THUR-muhl)—having to do with heat

READ MORE

Bell, Samantha. *Cool Military Gear*. Ready for Military Action. Minneapolis: Core Library, 2015.

Mitchell, Susan K. *Spy Gizmos and Gadgets*. The Secret World of Spies. Berkeley Heights, N.J.: Enslow Publishers, 2012.

INTERNET SITES

FactHound offers a safe, fun way to find Internet sites related to this book. All of the sites on FactHound have been researched by our staff.

Here's all you do:
Visit *www.facthound.com*
Type in this code: 9781515720317

INDEX

READ THEM ALL!

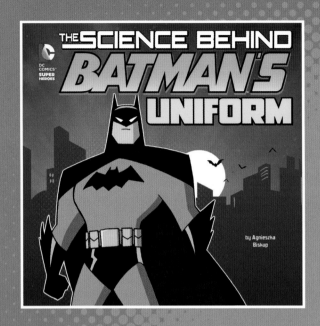

THE SCIENCE BEHIND BATMAN'S UNIFORM
by Agnieszka Biskup

THE SCIENCE BEHIND BATMAN'S GROUND VEHICLES
by Tammy Enz

THE SCIENCE BEHIND BATMAN'S FLYING MACHINES
by Tammy Enz

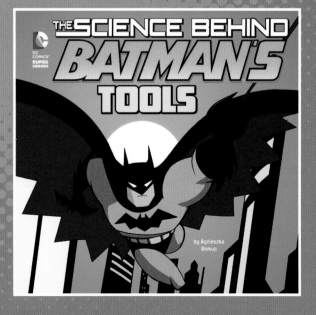

THE SCIENCE BEHIND BATMAN'S TOOLS
by Agnieszka Biskup